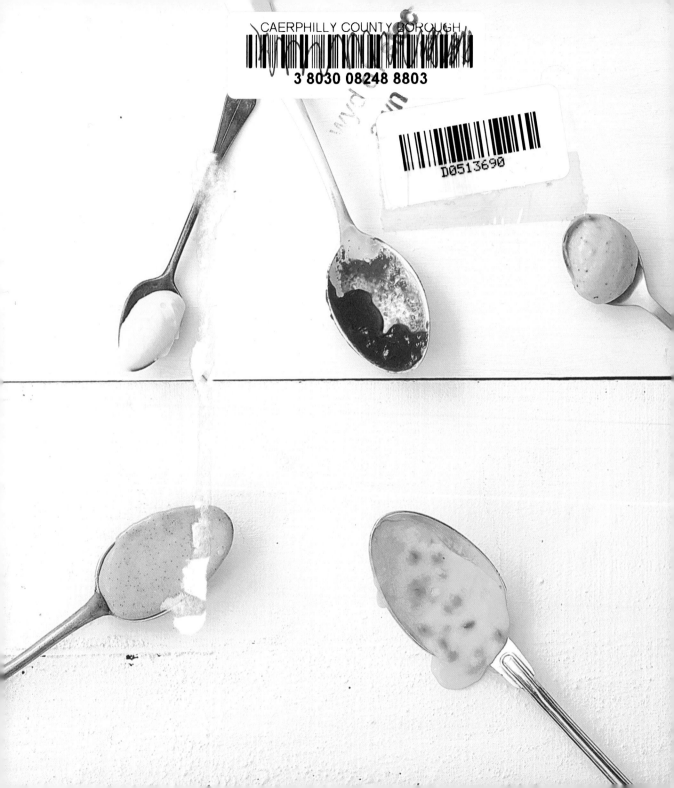

RACHEL KHOO'S
sweet & savoury pâtés

WEIDENFELD & NICOLSON

RACHEL KHOO'S
sweet & savoury pâtés

WEIDENFELD & NICOLSON

This edition published in Great Britain in 2014 by Weidenfeld & Nicolson
Originally published in 2010 by Hachette Livre -- Marabout
Text © Rachel Khoo 2014
Design and layout © Weidenfeld & Nicolson 2014
ISBN: 978 0 297 8 6895 8

10 9 8 7 6 5 4 3 2 1

Photography by Keiko Oikawa
Food styling by Rachel Khoo
Prop styling by Élodie Rambaud
Design by Kate Barr
English translation by Isabel Varea for Ros Schwartz Translations Ltd

The Orion Publishing Group's policy is to use papers that are natural, renewable
and recyclable and made from wood grown in sustainable forests. The logging
and manufacturing processes are expected to conform to the environmental
regulations of the country of origin.

Printed and bound in China.

Weidenfeld & Nicolson
The Orion Publishing Group Ltd
Orion House
5 Upper St Martin's Lane
London WC2H 9EA

An Hachette UK Company

www.orionbooks.co.uk

contents

The daughter of a Malaysian Chinese father and an Austrian mother, Rachel Khoo grew up in Croydon before graduating from Central Saint Martin's College of Art and Design in London. Her passion for patisserie lured her to Paris, where she studied at Le Cordon Bleu and became a pastry chef and cook.

First published in French as *Pates à Tartiner*, this was her second cookery book. Rachel's culinary life in Paris was the subject of the TV series and bestselling cookery book, *The Little Paris Kitchen*.

foreword

You may not think twice about a sweet or savoury spread when you have it on your toast in the morning but for me, there's nothing more enjoyable than to start the day with a little something homemade.

In an age where a day doesn't go past without a news report claiming that store-bought products contain ingredients that are best not consumed – there's no doubt about it, homemade rules. But that's not the only reason for making your own spread. A jar of homemade pâté (sweet or savoury) is the perfect way to wow friends and family (a pot of homemade lemon curd has often got me out of many a sticky situation).

Making your own sweet or savoury pâtés couldn't be simpler. This small book of recipes gives you a feast of ideas for delicious delights you can whip up in your kitchen. If you're a bit of a novice in the kitchen, there are plenty of easy-to-do recipes to kick off your culinary career.

A homemade pâté is not just for breakfast; it's a great way to spruce up your lunch box, satisfy your snack-time cravings, pimp up aperitif time or fulfill your midnight munchies.

Whether you have a sweet tooth and hunker after some chocolate and hazelnut spread or a craving for some buttery smooth chicken liver pâté, there's a recipe in this book to satisfy any craving.

five good reasons to make your own spreads

What better way to start your day than with a slice of toast and a generous dollop of your own homemade spread? The fact that you've made it yourself makes it that much more delicious.

one
Because they taste wonderful!
Just a little on a slice of bread is a real treat.

two
Because it's really very easy.
A few simple ingredients and they're ready in a flash.

three
Because they'll be all your own work.
You can create your own recipes from your favourite ingredients.
And, of course, you know what you are eating – no more artificial flavours,
additives or preservatives.

four
Because they are delicious at any time of day:
breakfast, brunch, teatime or as an appetiser.
Mix them with yogurt, spread them on pancakes, a lovely
fresh baguette or piping hot blinis – a mini feast in a jiffy!

five
Because they make great gourmet gifts.
Bottle and label them as a treat for loved ones.

THE BASICS

the basics

*Making spreads is dead easy. The key is to use top-quality ingredients.
You only need a few products to put a spread together, and choosing them
with care will make all the difference. Here are a few hints to start you off.*

chocolate

You'll get much better results with cooking chocolate or a dessert chocolate
with a high cocoa content than with a cheap brand. Some specialist shops
sell cooking chocolate in the form of drops; with drops you don't have to
chop the chocolate into pieces and it will melt more easily.

Of course, you can vary the kinds of chocolate that you use – dark, white or milk.
They are all quite different, but the results with each will be just as good.

sugar

White caster sugar is best for making caramel as you can keep a close eye on
the process. I like to make caramel with my homemade vanilla sugar. (To make
this, simply split a vanilla pod in two and place it in a jar with 500g/1lb 2oz of sugar.
Leave it to stand for two weeks, stirring about twice a week. Store in a cool, dry place.)

Some recipes require preserving sugar, which contains pectin – a natural gelling
agent that helps the spread to set and prevents it from being too runny. Preserving
sugar is readily available in supermarkets.

nuts & seeds

Walnuts, hazelnuts, almonds, cashews, pistachios and peanuts all
work well in spreads, as do sesame, sunflower and pumpkin seeds.

Buy whole, unsalted nuts, preferably peeled, for these recipes. Avoid powders, such
as almond or hazelnut – they are short on taste and contain fewer natural oils because
they have been stored for longer. If you grind your own nuts, your spread
will be richer, more even-textured and tastier.

Take care to check use-by dates and make sure that products are in
hermetically sealed packaging. Keep sachets in a cool,
dry place, preferably in the refrigerator or freezer.

To save having to prepare nuts, you can use nut oils, such as walnut
or almond. In wholefood or specialist shops you can also buy nut purée
or paste that you can use instead of actual nuts. Most of these are 100 per cent nut,
but some are already sweetened. If so, reduce the amount of sugar stated
in the recipe or, if you prefer, leave it out altogether.

fruit & vegetables

For a spread with a really intense flavour, go for very fresh, seasonal
fruit and vegetables. Otherwise, use frozen.

EQUIPMENT & UTENSILS

equipment & utensils

Unlike shop-bought spreads, the recipes in this book contain no artificial preservatives, so their shelf-life varies. The higher the sugar content, the longer they will keep, as sugar is a natural preservative. However, if the spread contains dairy products or eggs it will not keep as long.

Some spreads don't need to be stored in the refrigerator. Those that are refrigerated are sometimes a bit difficult to spread as they are chilled. Simply warm them slightly before eating.

jam jars

The best way to preserve spreads is to bottle them in jars, as the smells of the ingredients and the fat they contain don't linger in glass as they tend to do in plastic containers.

Jars must be sterilised to prevent the growth of bacteria or mould. To do this, wash them in soapy water and rinse well. Then stand them, without lids, in a cool oven at 130°C/250°F/gas mark ½ for 15–20 minutes.

blender

Some recipes require you to use a blender or food processor. With a domestic blender, the texture of your spreads will not be as smooth as they would be with a professional one, but they will certainly be as tasty.

If your food processor overheats when chopping nuts, stop it for a minute to let it cool down, otherwise the flavour and quality of the spread will be affected.

sieve

Use a jelly bag or a fine nylon sieve to sift fruit and remove skin and pips. Avoid metal sieves which tend to spoil the flavour of the fruit. If you don't have a nylon sieve, a nylon coffee filter will do the trick.

CHOCOLATE

classic chocolate spread

What can I say? I don't know anyone who can resist a slice of toast with a generous helping of chocolate spread. It only takes a few minutes to prepare and will tickle the taste buds of children and grown-ups alike.

makes about 400g/14oz • preparation time: 5 minutes • cooking time: 5 minutes

Pinch of salt
200ml/7fl oz single cream
200g/7oz dark chocolate, chopped into small pieces
50g/1¾oz softened butter, diced

Add the salt to the cream and bring to the boil.

Pour the boiling cream over the chocolate and butter. Wait 2 minutes before mixing them together. If any lumps remain, gently reheat in a heatproof bowl placed over a saucepan of gently simmering water or give it 30 seconds in the microwave.

Keep covered in the refrigerator and eat within 2 weeks.

tips & variations

Take the chocolate spread out of the refrigerator at least 10 minutes before using. It will be easier to spread at room temperature. If it's still too hard, stand the jar in a bowl of hot water for a few minutes or gently reheat in the microwave.

If dark chocolate isn't your cup of tea, replace half with milk chocolate. Your spread will still have the rich taste of dark chocolate, but will be slightly less bitter – just the way I prefer it. If you use only milk chocolate, add just 180ml/6fl oz of cream. The spread will take a little longer to set this way.

26

chocolate

dark chocolate
with one flavour

dark chocolate with spices

Pinch of salt
1 tsp ground cinnamon
½ tsp ground ginger
Pinch of nutmeg
2 cardamom seeds, crushed
200ml/7fl oz single cream
200g/7oz dark chocolate, chopped into small pieces
50g/1¾oz softened butter, diced

Add the salt and spices to the cream before bringing it to the boil.
Then follow the recipe for Classic Chocolate Spread (see page 24).

dark chocolate with mocha

140ml/5fl oz single cream
60ml/2fl oz strong espresso
Pinch of salt
100g/3½oz dark chocolate, chopped into small pieces
100g/3½oz milk chocolate, chopped into small pieces
50g/1¾oz softened butter, diced

Bring the cream to the boil with the espresso and salt.
Then follow the recipe for Classic Chocolate Spread (see page 24).

dark chocolate with liquorice

½ tsp liquorice powder (available from specialist shops)
Pinch of salt
200ml/7fl oz single cream
200g/7oz dark chocolate, chopped into small pieces
50g/1¾oz softened butter, diced

Stir the liquorice and salt into the cream before bringing it to the boil.
Then follow the recipe for Classic Chocolate Spread (see page 24).

dark chocolate with mint

200ml/7fl oz single cream
4 hard-boiled peppermint sweets
Pinch of salt
200g/7oz dark chocolate, chopped into small pieces
50g/1¾oz softened butter, diced

Simmer the cream with the peppermint sweets and salt. Stir frequently
until the mints have melted, then bring to the boil. Pour the boiling
cream over the chocolate and butter. Wait 2 minutes before stirring.
Then follow the recipe for Classic Chocolate Spread (see page 24).

dark chocolate
with one flavour

dark & milk chocolate with Earl Grey tea

Pinch of salt
2 tbsp loose Earl Grey tea (or 2 tea bags)
240ml/8 ½ fl oz whole single cream
100g/3 ½ oz dark chocolate, chopped into small pieces
100g/3 ½ oz milk chocolate, chopped into small pieces
50g/1 ¾ oz softened butter, diced

Add the salt and tea to the cream and bring to the boil.

Turn off the heat and leave to infuse for 10 minutes. Remove the
tea leaves or tea bags, return the cream to the boil and pour over
the chocolate and butter. Wait 2 minutes before stirring.

Then follow the recipe for Classic Chocolate Spread (see page 24).

classic white chocolate spread

Among purists, there's some controversy over white chocolate. Some even claim it isn't chocolate at all. Consisting only of sugar, cocoa butter, milk and some flavourings, it doesn't contain any actual cocoa. Of course, that doesn't make it any less delicious.

*makes 400g/14oz • preparation time: 5 minutes •
standing time: 15 minutes • cooking time: 15 minutes*

250g/9oz white chocolate, chopped into small pieces
150ml/5fl oz single cream
Pinch of salt

Melt the chocolate in a heatproof bowl placed over a saucepan of gently simmering water, stirring from time to time. Once the chocolate has melted, stir in the cream and salt. If any lumps remain, reheat the water to a simmer, then replace the bowl containing the mixture over the saucepan of water and stir until smooth.

Cover and leave to cool in the refrigerator for 15 minutes. The spread will keep for 2 weeks refrigerated.

white chocolate with one flavour

white chocolate with vanilla

1 vanilla pod
150ml/5fl oz single cream
Pinch of salt
250g/9oz white chocolate, chopped into small pieces

Split the vanilla pod in 2 and scrape out the seeds. Put the cream in a saucepan with
the salt, vanilla pod and seeds and bring to the boil. Leave to infuse
for 10 minutes and remove the vanilla pod. Then follow the recipe for
Classic White Chocolate Spread (see page 32).

white chocolate with lavender

150ml/5fl oz single cream
Pinch of salt
1 tsp dried lavender
250g/9oz white chocolate, chopped into small pieces

Put the cream in a saucepan with the salt and lavender and bring to the boil.
Leave to infuse for 10 minutes. Pour the cream through a sieve to remove the
lavender. Then follow the recipe for Classic White Chocolate Spread (see page 32).

white chocolate with matcha

Pinch of salt
150ml/5fl oz single cream
2 tsp matcha (finely milled or powdered green tea)
250g/9oz white chocolate, chopped into small pieces

Add the salt to the cream and bring to the boil. Stir in the matcha and whisk the mixture. Then follow the recipe for Classic White Chocolate Spread (see page 32).

white chocolate with tonka bean*

½ tonka bean
150ml/5fl oz whole single cream
Pinch of salt
250g/9oz white chocolate, chopped into small pieces

Finely grate the tonka bean. Add it to the cream with the salt, boil for 2 minutes and set aside. Then follow the recipe for Classic White Chocolate Spread (see page 32).
A tonka bean is sometimes used as a substitute for vanilla and is commonly used in French cuisine.

white chocolate with orange

150ml/5fl oz single cream
Pinch of salt
Zest of 1 organic or unwaxed orange, finely grated
250g/9oz white chocolate, chopped into small pieces
4 tbsp candied orange slices, chopped into small pieces

Bring the cream to the boil with the salt and grated orange zest, then follow the recipe for Classic White Chocolate Spread (see page 32). Leave the spread to rest in the refrigerator for 15 minutes, then stir in the candied orange.

chocolate

chocolate
with olive oil

An astonishingly delectable combination! Choose extra virgin olive oil from the first pressing for its more pronounced flavour of olives and slightly peppery taste.

makes 300g/10½oz • preparation time: 5 minutes • cooking time: 10 minutes

200g/7oz white or dark chocolate
Pinch of salt
100ml/3 ½ fl oz extra virgin olive oil

Put the chocolate and salt in a heatproof bowl and place over a saucepan of gently simmering water. Stir from time to time until the chocolate has melted.

Slowly pour the olive oil over the chocolate, stirring constantly. Transfer the spread to a sterilised jar and seal. The spread will take 30 minutes to set in the refrigerator or 2 hours at room temperature. It will keep for about a week in a cool, dark place.

variations
Walnut, pistachio or hazelnut oils also combine very well with chocolate. They add flavour to the spread without the tedious process of grinding the nuts. Another advantage of using nut oils is that you can make spreads suitable for people who are allergic to dairy products.

OLIVE

NUT

nutty chocolate spread

This is the homemade version of the famous chocolate spread. Everyone knows the popular Italian chocolate and hazelnut kind. Unlike the versions you find in supermarkets though, this version contains no artificial preservatives or flavourings, plus it is much more chocolatey.

makes about 300g/10½oz • preparation time: 10 minutes • cooking time: 10 minutes

150g/5½oz whole hazelnuts (or other nuts), skinned
150g/5½oz dark, milk or white chocolate, chopped into small pieces
2 tbsp sunflower oil
2 tbsp icing sugar
½ tsp pure vanilla essence
Pinch of salt

Preheat the oven to 180°C/350°F/gas mark 4. Spread the nuts over a baking sheet and toast them for 10 minutes, until golden. Leave to cool for a while.

Meanwhile, melt the chocolate in a heatproof bowl placed over a saucepan of gently simmering water, stirring from time to time. Grind the nuts until you have a fine consistency in a food processor. Add the oil, icing sugar, vanilla essence and salt, and continue to blend to a smooth paste. Stir the chocolate into the mixture.

This spread can be stored unopened in a cool place, away from light. Make sure the jar has been sterilised (see page 21) and that the lid is airtight.

Store in the refrigerator after opening. If kept in the refrigerator, remove 30 minutes before using or soften by placing the jar in hot water or microwaving for 30 seconds.

Other nuts, such as almonds, macadamias, peanuts, pistachios and cashews combine wonderfully well with chocolate. You can also add flavour to the spread with orange zest, cinnamon, ginger, etc.

if you don't have a food processor …
… you can use nut purée instead. There are lots to choose from, including almond, hazelnut, cashew, peanut, etc. in health-food shops.

If the purée comprises 100 per cent nuts, use the same quantity of purée as you would whole nuts. Some nut purées also contain sugar, salt or vanilla. If so, simply mix the purée and the melted chocolate with 2 tbsp sunflower oil.

praline spread

Nuts and chocolate are already a winning combination, but praline gives this spread a little something extra, making the mixture deliciously crunchy.

makes about 550g/1lb 4oz • preparation time: 10 minutes • cooking time: 20 minutes

150ml/5fl oz single cream
Pinch of salt
100g/3½oz dark chocolate, chopped into small pieces

praline
150g/5¾oz sugar
50ml/1½fl oz water
100g/3½oz blanched hazelnuts
100g/3½oz blanched almonds

Line a large baking sheet with greaseproof paper. To make the praline, dissolve the sugar in the water in a large saucepan. When the mixture comes to the boil, add the nuts. Stir constantly for 10–15 minutes to prevent the nuts from sticking or burning. When the mixture is a dark, golden caramel colour, spread it over the prepared baking sheet. Leave to cool for 15 minutes.

Meanwhile, bring the cream and salt to the boil and pour over the chocolate. Wait 2 minutes before stirring, then set aside. Break the praline into 3 pieces and put them through a blender, one piece at a time to produce a fine powder. If you prefer a crunchier spread, blend for a shorter time.

Stir the praline into the chocolate spread. The spread will keep for about 2 weeks covered in the refrigerator.

crunchy chocolate
spread

*It couldn't be simpler to achieve a nice crunchy effect. You'll need a rolling pin,
a freezer bag and the crunchy ingredient of your choice; maybe a honey and
sesame cereal bar, Maltesers, butterscotch, biscuits, nougatine, chopped nuts,
cacao nibs, puffed rice – it's up to you!*

*makes 500g / 1lb 2oz • preparation time: 10 minutes •
cooking time: 5 minutes*

using dark or milk chocolate
Pinch of salt
200ml/7fl oz single cream
200g/7oz chocolate, chopped
into small pieces
50g/1¾oz softened butter, diced

using white chocolate
250g/9oz chocolate, chopped
into small pieces
150ml/5fl oz single cream
Pinch of salt

the crunch
150g/5½oz of crunchy ingredient
(see above)

if using dark or milk chocolate
Add the salt to the cream and bring to the boil. Pour the cream over the
chocolate and butter. Wait 2 minutes before stirring. Refrigerate for 10 minutes.

if using white chocolate
Melt the chocolate in a heatproof bowl over a saucepan of gently simmering water.
Stir from time to time. Stir in the cream and salt. If any lumps remain, gently reheat
the mixture as in the previous step. Refrigerate for 10 minutes.

both versions
Put the crunchy ingredient of your choice in a freezer bag, wrap the bag in a tea towel,
then use a rolling pin to crush into small pieces. Stir into the cooled spread.

nut

peanut butter

I was raised on peanut butter and honey sandwiches. It wasn't only just a treat; nuts are also loaded with omega-3 fatty acids. You can also try using seeds – sesame, pumpkin or sunflower seeds work really well with this recipe. In Middle Eastern cuisine, sesame paste – otherwise known as tahini – is widely used for making hummus and pastries.

makes 300g/10½oz • preparation time: 10 minutes • cooking time: 10 minutes

280g/10oz unsalted peanuts (or other unsalted nuts or seeds), shelled
½ tsp salt (or to taste)
4 tbsp sunflower oil (or a little more to taste)
1 tsp honey or maple syrup (or to taste)

Preheat the oven to 180°C/350°F/gas mark 4. Spread the peanuts on a baking sheet and toast them in the oven for 10 minutes, then leave to cool. Grind the peanuts to a fine powder in a food processor, then add the salt, oil and honey or maple syrup.

Continue to blend, adding more oil if necessary to make an easily spreadable paste. Scrape the bottom and sides of the food processor to ensure the ingredients are thoroughly mixed. If you prefer a crunchier texture, add a handful of chopped nuts at the end.

This type of spread is best stored in an airtight container in the refrigerator.

variations

Peanuts aren't your only option. You can use almonds, macadamia nuts, Brazil nuts, hazelnuts, cashews, pistachios – the list is endless. According to the quality and type of nuts or seeds you use, you may need more or less sunflower oil. Adjust the quantity as you go.

nut

crème de marrons

I fell in love with crème de marrons on my first trip to Paris. At the time, this chestnut spread looked so exotic that I couldn't wait to taste it. I tried some out on a pancake – simply scrumptious.

makes 300g / 10 ½ oz • preparation time: 5 minutes • cooking time: 15 minutes

1 vanilla pod, split in 2
180ml/6fl oz single cream
200g/7oz chestnuts, bottled, frozen or tinned
25g/1oz soft brown sugar
1 ½ tbsp cognac (optional)

Scrape the seeds out of the vanilla pod and put them in a saucepan with the pod and the cream. Add all the other ingredients. Simmer over a low heat for 15 minutes, stirring from time to time.

Leave to cool. Remove the vanilla pod then blend to a smooth paste. If it seems too thick or too hard, blend in a little more cream.

Crème de marrons will keep covered in the refrigerator for at least 2 weeks.

nougat spread

*The crunchiness of the nuts, the sweetness of the honey and the
nougat texture all make this spread something to savour by the spoonful.*

*makes 350g/12oz • preparation time: 20 minutes •
cooking time: 10 minutes*

50g/1¾oz almonds, shelled and unsalted
50g/1¾oz hazelnuts, shelled and unsalted
150g/5½oz honey
2 egg whites
25g/1oz pistachios, shelled and unsalted
20g/¾oz glacé cherries

Preheat the oven to 180°C/350°F/gas mark 4. Roast the almonds and hazelnuts
(not the pistachios) for 10 minutes. Leave to cool.

Heat the honey in a saucepan over a medium heat until it reaches 115°C/239°F.
(If you don't have a thermometer, drop a teaspoon of the honey into cold water.
It should form a soft ball.)

Meanwhile, whip the egg whites until they peak. Slowly add the honey to the
egg whites while continuing to whip the mixture. Continue to beat at high
speed for about 6 minutes until it thickens.

Coarsely chop the pistachios and cherries and stir them into the nougat.
This spread is best eaten immediately as it will dry up if left for too long.

CARAMEL

classic dulce de leche

No one really knows the exact origin of dulce de leche, but it is widely used in French and Latin-American cuisine – in Spanish, the name translates to 'milk jam'. One thing is for sure though – it's highly addictive.

makes about 250g/9oz • preparation time: 10 minutes • cooking time: 1½–2 hours

1 vanilla pod, split in two
1 litre/1¾ pints of whole milk

300g/10½oz sugar
½ tsp fleur de sel

Scrape the seeds out of the vanilla pod and put them in a large saucepan with the pod, milk, sugar and fleur de sel. Place over a medium heat and whisk constantly until the mixture comes to the boil. Reduce the heat, so that the mixture is barely simmering, then cook, uncovered, for 1½ hours, stirring at regular intervals. If in doubt, turn the heat down even lower – the milk shouldn't boil, otherwise a skin may form on the surface.

Check the consistency after 1½ hours. The milk should have reduced and turned a pale caramel colour. For a more liquid result, stop cooking a little sooner; for a thicker mixture for spreading or as a filling for biscuits, cook a little longer. Bear in mind that it will continue to thicken as it cools. Discard the vanilla pod before using. Dulce de leche will keep for about 2 weeks in the refrigerator.

easy dulce de leche

400g/14oz sweetened condensed milk
1 vanilla pod, split in 2
½ tsp salt

Preheat the oven to 220°C/425°F/gas mark 7. Pour the condensed milk into a shallow, glass dish. Stir in the vanilla seeds (discard the pod) and salt. Cover with aluminium foil. Place the covered dish in a second, larger dish or pan (containing enough water to reach halfway up the sides of the covered dish) and cook in the oven for 2 hours. Remove from the oven – it should by now be a lovely dark caramel colour – and leave to cool.

classic
caramel spread

This recipe is like the dulce de leche, but much quicker to prepare.
Don't be afraid to create your own version with spices or other flavourings.

makes 350g/12oz • preparation time: 5 minutes •
cooking time: 10 minutes

225g/8oz sugar
100ml/3½fl oz water
120ml/4fl oz single cream
Pinch of salt
100g/3½oz softened butter, diced

Put the sugar and water in a large saucepan and heat gently, stirring from
time to time as the caramel turns golden. Add the cream and salt. Take care as
the caramel may splash. Bring to the boil then let it bubble for 5 minutes, stirring
at 1-minute intervals. You should get a thick, dark, golden-brown caramel. Keep
careful watch when it begins to colour as it can burn very quickly.

Once the caramel mixture has achieved the right colour (dark golden, but not
black) and has thickened to the desired consistency, take it off the heat immediately
and continue to stir until it is barely simmering. Leave to stand for 10–15 minutes
in the refrigerator. Beat the butter until creamy then stir into the cooled caramel.
Pour the caramel into a sterilised jar.

This spread will keep in the refrigerator for about 2 weeks. If the caramel spread
is too hard when you take it out of the refrigerator, gently reheat before eating,
either in a heatproof bowl placed over a saucepan of gently simmering water or
give it 30 seconds in the microwave.

flavoured caramels

caramel with salted butter

225g/8oz sugar
100ml/3½fl oz water
120ml/4fl oz single cream
1 tsp fleur de sel
100g/3½oz softened butter, diced

Follow the recipe for Classic Caramel Spread (see page 60),
adding the fleur de sel with the cream.

caramel with apple & calvados

225g/8 oz sugar
100ml/3½fl oz water
100ml/3½fl oz apple juice
25ml/1fl oz Calvados
Pinch of salt
100g/3½oz softened butter, diced

Follow the recipe for Classic Caramel Spread (see page 60),
adding the apple juice and Calvados instead of the cream.

caramel with citrus fruit

225g/8oz sugar
120ml/4fl oz water
100ml/3½fl oz freshly squeezed citrus fruit juice
Pinch of salt
100g/3½oz softened butter, diced
Zest of 1 citrus fruit

Follow the recipe for Classic Caramel Spread (see page 60),
adding the citrus juice instead of the cream. Stir in the zest at the end.

caramel with whisky

225g/8oz sugar
100ml/3½fl oz water
Pinch of salt
100g/3½oz softened butter, diced
100ml/3½fl oz single cream
25ml/1fl oz whisky

Follow the recipe for Classic Caramel Spread (see page 60),
adding the whisky at the same time as the cream.

Noix de coco

Pain d'épices

Fleur de sel

Whisky

caramel with gingerbread spices

225g/8oz sugar
100ml/3½fl oz water
120ml/4fl oz single cream
Pinch of salt
100g/3½oz softened butter, diced
1 tsp ground cinnamon
½ tsp ground ginger
¼ tsp ground cloves
¼ tsp ground coriander
¼ tsp ground nutmeg

Follow the recipe for Classic Caramel Spread (see page 60),
adding the spices at the end.

caramel with coconut

225g/8oz sugar
100ml/3½fl oz water
225ml/8fl oz coconut milk
Pinch of salt
3 tbsp desiccated coconut (optional)

Follow the recipe for Classic Caramel Spread (see page 60), but use the
coconut milk instead of the cream and omit the butter. If using the coconut,
sprinkle before serving.

FRUIT

lemon curd
& other citrus fruit curds

Curds are sweet spreads, mostly based on citrus fruit. They comprise beaten eggs, sugar, fruit juice and zest, cooked over a low heat until they thicken. They are then left to cool to form a soft, even-textured spread with an intense flavour.

makes 450g/1lb • *preparation time: 15 minutes* • *cooking time: 20 minutes*

3 lemons (or 4 limes, 1 medium-sized pink grapefruit or 2 oranges), organic or unwaxed

200g/7oz sugar

3 eggs

Pinch of salt

100g/3½oz softened butter, diced

Using a lemon zester, remove the zest from the fruit before squeezing them – you need about 120ml/4fl oz of juice.

In a medium-sized saucepan, whisk together the juice, zest, sugar, eggs and salt. Then add the butter and place the saucepan over a low heat, whisking constantly until the butter has melted. Turn up the heat and cook, still whisking constantly, until the mixture thickens to a smooth, creamy consistency. The curd is ready when it coats the back of a spoon.

Pass the curd immediately through a sieve then pour it into an airtight container or a sterilised jar. The curd keeps for about 3 weeks in the refrigerator.

lemon curd with honey & cardamom

For this deliciously spicy and fragrant variation, replace 50g/1¾oz of sugar with 50g/1¾oz of honey. Follow the recipe above and at the same time as mixing all the ingredients together in the saucepan, add 3 crushed cardamom pods.

71

passion fruit curd

makes 450g/1lb • *preparation time:* **15 minutes** • *cooking time:* **20 minutes**

6 large passion fruits
200g/7oz sugar
3 eggs
Pinch of salt
100g/3½oz softened butter, diced

Cut the passion fruits open, scrape out the seeds and pulp and put in a saucepan with the sugar, eggs and salt. Whisk together, then place over a low heat.

Add the butter and continue to whisk until it has melted.

Turn up the heat and whisk constantly until the mixture thickens to a smooth and creamy consistency. The curd is ready when it coats the back of a spoon.

Pour into an airtight container or a sterilised jar.
Passion fruit curd keeps for about 3 weeks in the refrigerator.

raspberry &
black pepper curd

The flavour of black pepper goes wonderfully well with raspberries. Use whole peppercorns to truly appreciate this perfect match.

Real pepper fans should try it with long peppers. An essential ingredient in antiquity, it was later superseded by round, black peppercorns. Long pepper is less piquant, with a flavour reminiscent of liquorice.

*makes 450g/1lb • preparation time: **15 minutes** • cooking time: **20 minutes***

300g/10½oz raspberries, fresh or frozen
2 tbsp water
200g/7oz sugar
3 eggs, beaten
1 tsp freshly ground ground black pepper
100g/3½oz softened butter, diced
Pinch of salt

Heat the raspberries, water, sugar, eggs, pepper and salt in a saucepan on a low heat. When the raspberries have begun to disintegrate and the mixture is beginning to boil, add the butter. Continue to whisk until the butter has melted.

Turn up the heat and whisk constantly until the mixture thickens to a smooth and creamy consistency. The curd is ready when it coats the back of a spoon.

Pass the curd immediately through a sieve, then pour into an airtight container or a sterilised jar. Raspberry curd keeps for about 3 weeks in the refrigerator.

kaya

'Kaya' is the Malay word for coconut jam, which is very popular in South-East Asia. It can be served as a spread on breakfast toast, mixed with rice pudding or spread on cakes.

makes 350g/12oz • preparation time: 5 minutes • cooking time: 20 minutes

½ vanilla pod
200ml/7fl oz coconut milk
4 egg yolks
200g/7oz soft brown sugar
Pinch of salt

Scrape out the seeds from the vanilla pod and place them in a saucepan with the vanilla pod and the rest of the ingredients. Stir well.

Place the saucepan over a low heat and cook for 15–20 minutes, stirring constantly until the mixture thickens. Pass the mixture immediately through a sieve.

Leave to cool a little before pouring it into an airtight container or a sterilised jar. Kaya keeps for about 3 weeks in the refrigerator.

fruit

sirop de Liège

Real sirop de Liège is produced in the Liège region of Belgium. My version of the thick caramel syrup with apples and pears comes very close to the original.

makes about 450g/1lb • preparation time: 15 minutes • cooking time: 1 hour 30 minutes

500g/1lb 2oz apples
1kg/2¼lb pears
50ml/1¾fl oz water
1 vanilla pod, split in 2
Pinch of salt
200g/7oz sugar

Peel then cut the apples and pears into eighths, reserving the cores and the peel. Put the fruit, including the cores and peel, in a saucepan with the other ingredients, except the sugar. Cover and cook on a low heat for 1 hour, stirring from time to time.

Pass the mixture through a sieve. Don't press too hard or you will end up with a fruit compote. Pour the mixture into a large saucepan with the sugar. Simmer over a low heat for 30 minutes so that the mixture turns syrupy – it will thicken as it cools.

Pour the syrup into a sterilised jar and make sure the lid is airtight. If unopened and stored in a dark place, the syrup will keep for at least 6 months. Once opened, it will keep for 1 month in the refrigerator.

fruit

plum & rosemary syrup

makes about 450g/1lb • *preparation time: 15 minutes* •
cooking time: 1 hour 30 minutes

500g/1lb 2oz apples
1kg/2¼lb plums
50ml/1¾fl oz water
2 sprigs of rosemary
Pinch of salt
200g/7oz sugar

Peel then cut the apples and plums into eighths, reserving the apple core and peel. Put the fruit, including the core and peel, in a saucepan with the other ingredients, except the sugar. Cover and cook over a low heat for 1 hour, stirring from time to time.

Pass the mixture through a sieve. Don't press too hard or you will end up with a fruit compote. Pour the mixture into a large saucepan with the sugar. Simmer over a low heat for 30 minutes so that the mixture turns syrupy – it will thicken as it cools.

Pour the syrup into a sterilised jar and make sure the lid is airtight. If unopened and stored in a dark place, the syrup will keep for at least 6 months. Once opened, it will keep for 1 month in the refrigerator.

cherry & basil syrup

makes about 450g/1lb • *preparation time:* **15 minutes** • *cooking time:* **1 hour 30 minutes**

500g/1lb 2oz apples
600g/1lb 5oz frozen cherries, stoned
50ml/1¾fl oz water
a bunch of basil
Pinch of salt
300g/10½oz sugar

Peel then cut the apples into eighths, reserving the core and peel, then cut the cherries in half. Put the fruit, including the core and peel, in a saucepan with the other ingredients, except the sugar. Cover and cook over a low heat for 1 hour, stirring from time to time.

Pass the mixture through a sieve. Don't press too hard or you will end up with a fruit compote. Pour the mixture into a large saucepan with the sugar. Simmer over a low heat for 30 minutes so that the mixture turns syrupy – it will thicken as it cools.

Pour the syrup into a sterilised jar and make sure the lid is airtight. If unopened and stored in a dark place, the syrup will keep for at least 6 months. Once opened, it will keep for 1 month in the refrigerator.

CHOCOLATE & ...

chocolate &
marshmallow whirl

Marshmallow spread is very popular in the United States, where it is used on bread, biscuits, cakes, etc. I prefer to mix it with chocolate to balance its very sweet flavour.

---

makes 400g/14oz • preparation time: 30 minutes • cooking time: 10 minutes

---

chocolate
200ml/7fl oz single cream
Pinch of salt
200g/6¾oz dark chocolate,
chopped into small pieces
50g/1¾oz softened butter, diced

marshmallow
150g/5½oz marshmallows
60g/2oz butter
60ml/2fl oz single cream

To make the chocolate paste, pour the cream into a saucepan, add the salt and bring to the boil. Pour the boiling cream over the chocolate and butter and wait 2 minutes before stirring. If any lumps remain, reheat gently in a heatproof bowl over a saucepan of simmering water. Once you have a smooth paste, leave to stand in the refrigerator for 15 minutes.

Place all the ingredients for the marshmallow paste in a saucepan over a medium heat and heat them slowly. Stir constantly until the marshmallow melts. Once you have a smooth paste, leave it to stand for 10 minutes in the refrigerator.

When both pastes are cold, but not yet set, pour a little of the chocolate paste into a sterilised jar, followed by a little of the marshmallow paste. Continue to fill the jar with alternate chocolate and marshmallow layers, then stir with a chopstick or a spoon handle to create a marbled effect.

This spread will keep in the refrigerator for about 2 weeks.

84

chocolate & ...

chocolate & mango whirl

A touch of chilli pepper adds a gentle kick to this chocolate and fruit spread.

makes 400g/14oz • preparation time: 15 minutes • cooking time: 10 minutes

mango
200g/7oz mango flesh
120g/4oz preserving sugar
2 tbsp water
1 tsp ground chilli pepper

chocolate
Pinch of salt
200ml/7fl oz single cream
200g/6¾oz dark chocolate, chopped into small pieces
50g/1¾oz softened butter, diced

To make the mango paste, mix the mango, preserving sugar, water and chilli pepper in a large saucepan over a medium heat and cover with a lid when the mixture comes to the boil. Simmer for 5 minutes before turning off the heat. Stir to a smooth paste then place in the refrigerator for 10 minutes. It should be cold, but not yet set.

To make the chocolate paste, add the salt to the cream and bring to the boil. Pour the boiling cream over the chocolate and butter and wait 2 minutes before stirring. If any lumps remain, gently reheat the paste in a heatproof bowl placed over a saucepan of gently simmering water.

Once the mixture is smooth, place in the refrigerator for 10 minutes. It should be cold, but not yet set. Pour a little chocolate paste into a sterilised jar, followed by a little mango paste. Continue to fill the jar with alternate mango and chocolate layers, then stir with a chopstick or a spoon handle to create a marbled effect.

The spread will keep in the refrigerator for about 2 weeks.

chocolate & ...

white chocolate
& raspberry whirl

The combination of raspberries and white chocolate is a feast for the eyes as well as the taste buds. The slight acidity of the raspberries is a perfect match for the creamy texture of the white chocolate.

---

makes 400g/14oz • preparation time: 10 minutes • cooking time: 20 minutes

---

white chocolate cream
130g/4½oz white chocolate, chopped into small pieces
70ml/2½fl oz single cream
Pinch of salt

raspberry jam
200g/7oz frozen raspberries
120g/4oz preserving sugar

To make the white chocolate cream, melt the chocolate in a heatproof bowl placed over a saucepan of gently simmering water. Stir occasionally, then add the cream and salt. If any lumps remain, keep the heatproof bowl, or inner container of the bain-marie, over the simmering water and stir until smooth.

Leave the paste to cool for 15 minutes in the refrigerator. It should be cold but not yet set. Mix the raspberries and preserving sugar in a large saucepan and cover with a lid when the mixture comes to the boil. Boil for 5 minutes before turning off the heat.

Leave to cool for 15 minutes in the refrigerator. The jam should be cold, but not yet set. Blend in a food processor for 2 minutes to remove some of the pips. Pour a little chocolate paste into a sterilised jar, followed by a little raspberry jam. Continue to fill the jar with alternate white chocolate and raspberry layers. Stir with a chopstick or a spoon handle to create a marbled effect.

This spread will keep for about 2 weeks in the refrigerator.

chocolate & ...

SAVOURY

tapenades

The word 'tapenade' comes from the Provençal tapéno, *meaning capers, so authentic tapenades always contain capers.*

makes about 300g/10½oz • preparation time: 15 minutes

classic tapenade

½ garlic clove, crushed
1 tbsp freshly squeezed lemon juice
3 anchovy fillets, chopped
3 tbsp capers, rinsed
175g/6oz black olives, pitted
1 small bunch of fresh parsley, chopped
2–4 tbsp extra virgin olive oil
Salt and freshly ground black pepper

To obtain a coarse texture, simply crush all the ingredients together in a pestle and mortar, adding sufficient oil to form a paste. Season to taste.

Tapenade will keep for 5 days in the refrigerator.

tip
For a smoother tapenade, blend the garlic, lemon juice, anchovies and capers in a food processor for about 30 seconds, then add the olives, parsley and enough oil until it forms a paste.

sun-dried tomato & ricotta tapenade

150g/5½oz ricotta
100g/3½oz sun-dried tomatoes
3 tbsp capers, rinsed
½ garlic clove, crushed
1 tbsp freshly squeezed lemon juice
1 small bunch of fresh parsley, chopped
½ tsp freshly ground black pepper

Blend all the ingredients to a paste in a food processor, adding the pepper last.

artichoke tapenade

½ garlic clove, peeled and chopped
100g/3½oz green olives, pitted
1 tbsp capers, rinsed
200g/7oz tinned artichoke hearts, drained and cut into quarters
1 tbsp freshly squeezed lemon juice
6 tbsp extra virgin olive oil
Salt and freshly ground black pepper
Pinch of chilli powder
Handful of shaved Parmesan (optional)

Add the garlic, olives, capers, artichoke hearts, lemon juice and olive oil one
by one to a food processor and blend to an almost smooth paste, with just a few
pieces remaining. Taste, then season with salt, pepper and chilli. If you like,
serve with some shaved Parmesan.

hummus

classic hummus

makes about 200g/7oz • preparation time: 15 minutes

200g/7oz tinned chickpeas, rinsed and drained
½ garlic clove, peeled and crushed
Few drops of lemon juice
2–4 tbsp extra virgin olive oil
1 tsp tahini (sesame paste – see peanut butter recipe, page 50)
1 tsp ground cumin
Fleur de sel
Freshly ground black pepper

Blend all the ingredients (besides the salt and pepper) in a food processor to a coarse paste. Season to taste. Hummus will keep for 5 days in an airtight container in the refrigerator.

beetroot hummus

makes about 300g/10½oz • preparation time: 15 minutes

150g/5½oz tinned chickpeas, rinsed and drained
1 large cooked beetroot (approximately 175g/6oz)
1 garlic clove, peeled and crushed
Few drops of lemon juice
2–4 tbsp extra virgin olive oil
1 tsp tahini (sesame paste – see Peanut Butter recipe, page 50)
1 tsp ground cumin
Fleur de sel
Salt and freshly ground black pepper

Blend all the ingredients (besides the salt and pepper) in a food processor to a coarse paste. Season to taste. It's best to eat beetroot hummus on the same day as you make it as the beetroot quickly discolours.

savoury

carrot hummus

makes about 200g/7oz • *preparation time:* **15 minutes**
cooking time: **1 hour**

2 large carrots, peeled and coarsely chopped
2–4 tbsp extra virgin olive oil
100g/3½oz tinned chickpeas, rinsed and drained
½ garlic clove, peeled and crushed
1 tsp freshly squeezed lemon juice
1 tsp tahini (sesame paste, see Peanut Butter recipe, page 50)
1 tsp ground cumin
Pinch of sugar
Fleur de sel
Salt and freshly ground black pepper

Preheat the oven to 200°C/400°F/gas mark 6. Arrange the carrots on
a baking sheet, drizzle with olive oil and roast in the oven for 1 hour.

Blend all the ingredients (besides the salt and pepper) in a food processor to a
coarse paste. Season to taste. This type of hummus will keep for 5 days in an airtight
container in the refrigerator.

roasted red pepper hummus

makes about 400g/14oz • *preparation time:* *15 minutes*
cooking time: *40 minutes*

3 large sweet red peppers, coarsely chopped
2–4 tbsp extra virgin olive oil
130g/4½oz tinned chickpeas, rinsed and drained
½ garlic clove, peeled and crushed
1 tsp freshly squeezed lemon juice
1 tsp tahini (sesame paste, see Peanut Butter recipe, page 50)
1 tsp ground cumin
Pinch of sugar
Fleur de sel
Salt and freshly ground black pepper

Preheat the oven to 200ºC/400ºF/gas mark 6. Spread the chopped peppers on
a baking sheet, drizzle with olive oil and roast in the oven for 40 minutes.

Blend all the ingredients (besides the salt and pepper) in a food processor to a
coarse paste. Season to taste. This type of hummus will keep for 5 days in an airtight
container in the refrigerator.

goat's cheese cream
with macadamia nuts

Francesca Unsworth, my culinary collaborator, prepared this for some of the dinner parties the two of us organised in Sydney, Australia. Needless to say, it was a great success.

makes 200g / 7oz • preparation time: 15 minutes • cooking time: 10 minutes

100g/3½oz blanched macadamia nuts
100g/3½oz goat's cheese
Salt and freshly ground black pepper

Preheat the oven to 180°C/350°F/gas mark 4. Roast the macadamia nuts for 5–10 minutes until golden. Leave to cool for a few minutes before reducing them to a fine powder in a blender.

Mix them with the goat's cheese and season with salt and pepper. This spread will keep for 5 days in an airtight container in the refrigerator.

tip
Macadamia nuts add unique flavour to this spread, but if you can't find any, it works just as well with almonds.

avocado cream
with almonds

This is simpler than the traditional guacamole recipe made with avocado, but just as tasty. The almonds add a subtle nutty flavour to the spread.

makes 200g/7oz • preparation time: 15 minutes • cooking time: 10 minutes

50g/1¾oz almonds
1 large ripe avocado
1 tbsp lime juice
Salt and freshly ground black pepper

Preheat the oven to 180°C/350°F/gas mark 4. Roast the almonds for 5–10 minutes until golden. Leave to cool for a few minutes before reducing them to a fine powder in a blender.

Mash the avocado and drizzle with lime juice. Mix the almonds and avocado together in a food processor to make a coarse paste. Season to taste with salt and pepper.

This spread is best eaten immediately as avocados tend to turn brown very quickly.

103

spicy lentil spread

*The wonderful smell of this spread is irresistible as it cooks. If you like your food
a little spicier, adjust the quantities of the curry and chilli powder to your taste.*

*makes about 200g/7oz • preparation time: 10 minutes •
cooking time: 20 minutes*

185g/6½oz red lentils
1 onion, cut into quarters
475ml/16½fl oz water
1 tbsp olive oil
1 garlic clove, crushed
1 tbsp curry powder
1 tsp ground cumin
½ tsp chilli powder
Pinch of salt

Put the lentils, onion and water into a saucepan. Cover and bring to the boil.
Turn down the heat and leave the mixture to simmer for 15–20 minutes until
the lentils are soft. Remove the onion and leave the lentils to cool.

Put the oil, garlic and spices into a small frying pan and fry for a few minutes
until the mixture gives off a spicy smell. Purée the lentils and spices in a food
processor to produce a smooth mixture. Season to taste.

This spread will keep for 5 days in an airtight container in the refrigerator.

chicken-liver pâté

Living in France, I've learned to love chicken-liver pâté. There's no nicer appetiser than pâté spread on a crispy baguette with some gherkins.

makes 300g/10½oz • preparation time: 15 minutes • cooking time: 10 minutes • standing time: 4 hours

90g/3oz softened butter
1 shallot, finely chopped
2 sprigs of thyme
2 bay leaves
2 garlic cloves, finely chopped
225g/8oz chicken livers, cleaned and trimmed
2 tsp Worcestershire sauce
1 tbsp cognac
freshly ground black pepper

Melt 2 tbsp of the butter in a large saucepan, then add the shallot, thyme, bay leaves and garlic. Cook until the mixture softens, but don't allow it to brown.

Add the chicken livers, Worcestershire sauce and cognac. Cook for 5 minutes until the livers are cooked, but still pink in the middle. Leave to stand for 5 minutes. Remove the bay leaves and thyme, then blend with the remaining butter. Add black pepper to taste.

Leave to stand in the refrigerator for at least 4 hours. Chicken-liver pâté will keep for 5 days in an airtight container in the refrigerator.

107

savoury

anchoïade
with figs & walnuts

This recipe brings a touch of sweetness and crunchiness to the traditional anchoïade.

makes 150g / 5 ½ oz • preparation time: 15 minutes • cooking time: 10 minutes

80g/3oz walnuts
5 anchovies, preserved in salt
4 dried figs, coarsely chopped
Zest of 1 orange
½ garlic clove, peeled
25ml/1fl oz extra virgin olive oil
Generous pinch of fleur de sel

Preheat the oven to 180°C/350°F/gas mark 4 and roast the walnuts for 15–20 minutes until golden. Rinse the anchovies and dry them on kitchen paper.

Put the anchovies in a mortar with the walnuts, figs, orange zest and garlic and grind them with a pestle until they form a coarse paste – almost a purée, but still with some solid pieces. You can achieve the same consistency in a blender. Add the olive oil. Stir thoroughly and season to taste.

Anchoïade will keep for 5 days in an airtight container in the refrigerator.

smoked salmon rillettes
with wasabi

Wasabi adds a Japanese touch to this classic pâté. Known as 'Japanese horseradish', this root can be bought as a powder or paste and is used as a spice in many dishes. Use sparingly though as it can be very strong.

makes about 450g/1lb • preparation time: 10 minutes

250g/9oz smoked salmon
200g/7oz fromage frais
1 tbsp wasabi powder or paste
4 tbsp sesame seeds (plus a little extra to garnish)
4 tbsp chopped cucumber (plus a little extra to garnish)

Put the smoked salmon, fromage frais and wasabi in a blender to produce a smooth paste. Taste and add a little more wasabi, if necessary.

Using a spatula, stir in the sesame seeds and cucumber. Garnish with the extra sesame seeds and cucumber before serving.

This spread will keep for 5 days in an airtight container in the refrigerator.

savoury

smoked mackerel rillettes
with lemon & herbs

Ready in a few minutes, this is also very good with peppered, smoked mackerel.

makes 450g/1lb • preparation time: 5 minutes

250g/9oz smoked mackerel, skin and bones removed
200g/7oz fromage frais
Zest and juice of ½ lemon
2 tbsp finely chopped flat-leaf parsley (plus a little extra to garnish)
2 tbsp finely chopped chives (plus a little extra to garnish)
Freshly ground black pepper

Flake the mackerel and mix all the ingredients together by hand.
Season with black pepper. If you prefer a smoother paste, use a blender.

Smoked mackerel rillettes will keep for 5 days in an airtight container
in the refrigerator.

minted petits pois spread

with preserved lemon

Peas with mint is a classic. The preserved lemon adds a little something extra to this traditional combination.

makes 250g/9oz • preparation time: 15 minutes • cooking time: 5 minutes

200g/7oz frozen petits pois
1 preserved lemon
½ garlic clove
1 bunch of mint
50g/1¾oz crème fraîche
Salt and freshly ground black pepper

Cook the peas for a few minutes in salted, boiling water. Drain, then rinse them in cold water to preserve their colour.

Finely chop the preserved lemon into small pieces and wash the mint. Put the peas through a blender with the garlic, mint and crème fraîche. Taste, then season.

Stir the lemon into the paste or sprinkle it over the spread before serving. It's best to eat this spread the same day, as mint gradually loses its vivid colour.

haricot bean spread
with pomegranate seeds

The creamy texture of the beans and sweet flavour of the pomegranate seeds work perfectly together. If you have time, use frozen beans.

makes 200g/7oz • preparation time: 15 minutes • cooking time: 5 minutes

200g/7oz tinned haricot or navy beans
½ garlic clove
2 tbsp lemon juice
2 tbsp olive oil
1 pomegranate
½ bunch of parsley, finely chopped
Salt and freshly ground black pepper

Strain the beans through a sieve and rinse under running water. Put the beans in a food-processor with the garlic, lemon juice and olive oil and blend to a smooth paste. Extract the seeds from the pomegranate. Stir some of them into the spread with the parsley, then season to taste. Sprinkle the remaining seeds over the spread before serving.

This spread is best eaten the same day, but it will keep for 1 or 2 days in an airtight container in the refrigerator.

tip

To extract the pomegranate seeds, cut off the top end of the fruit, then score the pomegranate skin five or six times from top to bottom. Plunge the pomegranate into a bowl filled with water and leave to soak for 5 minutes. Keep the fruit under water to prevent the juice from splashing and separate it into large chunks. Then use your fingers to detach the seeds from the skin and membrane. The seeds will sink to the bottom of the bowl, while the skin and membrane will float to the surface. Collect and drain the seeds, then dry them.

savoury